D0264908

THE CLINK
QUICK & EASY
COOKBOOK

Having the opportunity to help transform the lives of
men and women who are trying to turn their fortunes
around, and to witness the positive impact that has on
their immediate families, is the most rewarding aspect of
my role with the Ministry of Justice and The Clink

Alberto Crisci MBE
Founder of The Clink

THE **CLINK** QUICK **&** EASY COOKBOOK

All recipes by Al Crisci, unless otherwise credited

___CONTENTS___

___FOREWORDS___

Finlay Scott
Clink Chairman

Since the founding of The Clink more than six years ago, over 800 prisoners have completed our course, with an extraordinary success rate of 90%. Your support in buying this book will help us to train more inmates, not only in the business of catering, but also in the joy of creating delicious dishes.

The simple act of cooking is restorative. In training our students and helping them to find work, they also gain life skills, learn how to work as part of a team and discover how rewarding the preparation and serving of food can be.

I hope you find these recipes accessible, easy and tasty and that this book becomes a staple on your kitchen shelf. I also hope that, while you cook from this book, you are reminded of how you are helping us in our work to reduce reoffending and – in effect – reduce crime.

Bon appetit!

Albert Roux OBE, KFO
Clink Group Chef Ambassador

Following the success of our first Clink recipe book in 2015, we have created this new book, filled with quick and easy recipes from the charity's ambassadors, graduates of the training schemes and prisoners working in the restaurants.

I am honoured to be the Group Chef Ambassador for this incredible charity. Through its work, we are releasing fully trained, qualified and passionate chefs and service staff into the British hospitality industry. It fills me with amazement to witness the level of untapped talent that the charity discovers within the prison system.

Once their sentence is served, Clink graduates enter society with nationally recognised City & Guilds NVQs, which not only help when securing employment, but also build their confidence, motivation and pride.

The charity also supports each individual upon release, to help them successfully to reintegrate into the world and continue on their path of change.

The objective of this book is to raise awareness of the meaningful work of the charity in providing prisoners with the necessary skills, professional training and pastoral support required to turn their lives around and become an asset to the hospitality industry and to society as a whole.

All proceeds from the sale of this book go towards the expansion of The Clink Charity's prisoner training scheme, so we are able to transform even more lives.

I do hope that you enjoy this book as much as we have enjoyed putting it together.

___ABOUT THE CLINK___

MISSION 'Changing attitudes, transforming lives and creating second chances'

Christopher Moore KFO, Clink Chief Executive

The sole aim of The Clink Charity is to reduce reoffending rates by training and placing our graduates – upon their release from prison – into employment in the hospitality industry. Since launching in 2009, the charity has achieved incredible results.

Prisoners at the Clink Restaurants work a 40-hour week while taking City & Guilds NVQs. Those who have six to 18 months of their sentence left are carefully selected for the programme, training full-time to reach the required level to succeed in their chosen path.

We have trained more than 800 prisoners since 2009 and received two 'outstanding' reports from Ofsted, for work at HMP High Down and HMP Brixton.

Our dedicated full-time trainers work closely with each of the prisoners while they are training. Upon their release, our support workers help our graduates to find employment, and mentor them weekly for six to 12 months, to help them to reintegrate into society.

We currently operate four Clink Restaurants, at HMP High Down, HMP Cardiff, HMP Brixton and HMP Styal. Dining at one of our restaurants is a memorable experience; service is second to none and the menus are creatively designed around the changing seasons and local (or even Clink grown) produce. Each restaurant also offers facilities for corporate events and private dining.

In addition to the restaurants, we operate Clink Gardens and Clink Events. Prisoners work at the Clink Gardens at HMP High Down and HMP Send to achieve City & Guilds NVQs in horticulture. Fruit, vegetables and herbs from the gardens are delivered to the restaurants by a prisoner out on licence for the day, along with eggs from chickens and honey from beehives for which the prisoners are also responsible.

Clink Events provides catering beyond the prison walls and gives prisoners in training the chance to experience event catering.

We have 200 employers willing to take graduates, such as Hilton Hotels, Wahaca and Mosimann's. We've won more than 40 awards, including The Sustainable Restaurant Association 3 Star Award for all four restaurants. Our catering industry ambassadors include Albert Roux, Antonio Carluccio and Giorgio Locatelli, and many others.

The Clink Charity would like to have 20 training facilities in operation by the end of 2020. Reaching this target will see more than 1,000 trained and qualified Clink graduates enter employment each year.

The charity's work not only changes the lives of our graduates, but saves tax payers' money and makes society a safer place.

STARTERS, SALADS AND LIGHTER MEALS

___COURGETTE SOUP with RICOTTA and MINT ___

An elegant green colour with a beautiful fragrance of mint and basil. A real corker for summer.

SERVES 4___PREP 20 minutes___COOK 15 minutes___MATT TEBBUTT

INGREDIENTS

4 tbsp olive oil
2 garlic cloves, finely chopped
1 onion, sliced
1kg courgettes, chopped chunkily
leaves from a bunch of basil
600ml vegetable stock
100ml double cream
6 tbsp finely grated Parmesan
4 tbsp ricotta
leaves from a bunch of mint

METHOD

___Take a large saucepan and add the olive oil and garlic. Add the onion and courgettes, salt and basil. Cook for around 10 minutes, until softened.

___Pour in the stock and cream and bring back to the boil, then reduce the heat and simmer for a few minutes. Now remove three-quarters of the soup and blend it. Stir the blended soup back into the pan, with some of the Parmesan, taste and season.

___Serve in warmed bowls with some crumbled ricotta, torn mint and a little more Parmesan.

___DELICATE CAULIFLOWER LEAF and PECORINO SOUP___

Perhaps the ultimate way to avoid kitchen waste. Cauliflower leaves have a subtle, pleasing taste.

SERVES 4___PREP 20 minutes___COOK 1 hour___JULES HECKMAN HUGHES

INGREDIENTS

trimmings from 2 cauliflowers
25g unsalted butter
1 garlic clove, chopped
50g plain flour
vegetable stock, to cover
35g parsley
leftover mashed potato
pinch of cayenne pepper
25g pecorino, finely grated
squeeze of lemon juice
a few basil leaves

METHOD

___Strip the leaves from the cauliflowers and remove their thick ribs. Chop up the main cauliflower stalks.

___Melt the butter in a heavy-based pan and sweat the cauliflower leaves, stalks and garlic. Stir in the flour, mix in the stock and simmer until soft (around one hour).

___Add the parsley and cook for 30 seconds, then just enough potato to thicken and the cayenne. Season well.

___Blend, then add the pecorino and stir to melt. Taste and lift the flavours with lemon juice. Serve in warmed bowls scattered with basil, with hot crusty rolls.

___SMOKED SALMON and DILL PATE___

This always goes down well and is the work of mere moments.

SERVES 6___PREP 5 minutes___EDWINA GROSVENOR

INGREDIENTS
255g smoked salmon
110g cream cheese
2 tbsp double cream
juice of ½ lemon
2 tbsp chopped dill fronds
pinch of caster sugar
salt and pepper

METHOD
___Put all the ingredients in a blender and blend until smooth.
___Season with salt and pepper to taste, going easy on the salt as the smoked salmon is salty.
___Serve with crackers, Melba toast, or crudités for dipping.

___SMOKED SALMON with HORSERADISH CREAM___

A sophisticated short-cut with piquant, classic flavours. Make the cream as hot or mild as you like.

SERVES 6___PREP 15 minutes___JANE SANDERSON

INGREDIENTS
450g smoked salmon
50g shallots, finely chopped
25g very small capers,
    drained and rinsed
25g gherkins, finely chopped
2 hard-boiled eggs, finely grated
25g finely chopped parsley leaves
50g horseradish sauce
150g crème fraîche
cayenne pepper, to taste
lime wedges, to serve

METHOD
___Divide the salmon between six plates. Scatter the shallots, capers, gherkins, eggs and parsley around it.
___For the horseradish cream, mix the horseradish in a bowl with the crème fraîche, adding cayenne to taste (go carefully, it's hot). Spoon some on to each plate.
___Serve with lime wedges.

___GAZPACHO___

Make this when you find really good-quality, ripe tomatoes, bursting with freshness. Drink icy cold on a warm summer's day.

SERVES 4___PREP 15 minutes

INGREDIENTS
600g tomatoes
1 large red pepper, deseeded
½ cucumber, peeled
6 spring onions, trimmed
2 garlic cloves
1 tsp chopped basil leaves
4 tbsp extra virgin olive oil
1 tbsp white wine vinegar
salt and pepper

METHOD
___Nick the base of each tomato with a knife. Put them in a large heatproof bowl and boil a kettle. Cover the tomatoes with boiling water and count for 15 seconds; you should start to see the skins peeling off. Drain the tomatoes and slip off the skins. Quarter each and cut out the seeds (discard these).
___Put the skinned, deseeded tomatoes in a blender with half the roughly chopped pepper, cucumber and spring onions. Add the garlic, basil, oil and vinegar and blend until smooth. Blend in 150ml of iced water. Season to taste. Finely chop the remaining pepper, cucumber and spring onions.
___Serve the gazpacho ice-cold, seasoning well to taste again once it is chilled, with the finely chopped vegetables on top.

___CHILLED SPINACH and PEA SOUP___

Wonderfully spring-like and aromatic with tarragon.

SERVES 4___PREP 15 minutes___COOK 25 minutes___JULES HECKMAN HUGHES

INGREDIENTS
6 tbsp unsalted butter
4–5 leeks, white and light green parts only, sliced
salt and pepper
900g spinach, coarse stalks removed
1.25 litres chicken stock
50g tarragon leaves
700g frozen peas, defrosted

___CHILLED CARROT SOUP___

The fines herbes mousse here really sets off the sweetness of the soup.

Serves 6___PREP 15 minutes___COOK 1 hour___JULES HECKMAN HUGHES

INGREDIENTS

For the soup

10 carrots, chopped
1.5 litres carrot juice
2 tsp unsalted butter
2 tsp honey
pinch of curry powder
360ml double cream
salt and white pepper

For the mousse

60ml crème fraîche
2 chives, finely chopped
leaves from 2 sprigs each of
   parsley, chervil and tarragon,
   finely chopped

METHOD

___For the soup, put the carrots in a saucepan with 600ml of the carrot juice, the butter, honey and curry powder. Bring to a simmer, then reduce the heat and simmer until the liquid has evaporated and the carrots are very soft, about one hour. Add the cream and simmer for five minutes.

___Purée the soup with the remaining carrot juice. Pass it through a sieve into a bowl and season to taste. Cover and chill.

___For the mousse, whisk the crème fraîche in a bowl until stiff peaks form. Fold in the herbs.

___Divide the soup between chilled soup bowls and place a spoonful of mousse in the centre of each.

METHOD

___Melt the butter over a medium heat. Add the leeks and cook until soft and translucent, about 10 minutes. Season.

___Add the spinach and cook until wilted. Stir in the stock and simmer for six minutes; the soup should remain bright green. Add the tarragon and peas and cook for five minutes.

___Purée the soup until smooth. (You may need to work in batches.) Pass it through a sieve into a bowl and season to taste. Cover and chill. Serve in chilled bowls.

___TERRIFIC THAI SOUP___

The coriander pesto is a twiddle, but mandatory! It's the contrast that makes the whole thing.

SERVES 4___PREP 20 minutes___COOK 25 minutes___JULIE PEASGOOD

INGREDIENTS

For the soup

1 onion, chopped

olive oil, plus 1–2 tbsp more for the pesto

1 tbsp finely chopped or grated root ginger

about 1 tbsp Thai curry paste, or to taste

1 large butternut squash, peeled, deseeded
   and chopped

2 sweet potatoes, peeled and chopped

600ml vegetable stock (ideally Marigold)

400g can of light or regular coconut milk

salt and pepper

For the pesto

good-sized bunch of coriander

finely grated zest and juice of
   1 unwaxed lemon

2 small or 1 large garlic clove

METHOD

___In a large pan, soften the onion in a little oil, then add the ginger and cook for a few minutes. Next, add the curry paste, fry for a minute or so, then stir in the squash and sweet potatoes. Pour in the stock, bring to a simmer and cook for 15 minutes, until the vegetables are tender. Blend (leaving it a bit chunky), then put it back in the pot and add the coconut milk. Warm through.

___Meanwhile, put the bunch of coriander (with stalks) in a blender with the lemon zest and juice, the garlic and 1–2 tbsp olive oil. Blend together.

___Check the seasoning and serve the soup in warmed bowls with good dollops of the pesto.

____ROCKET, MOZZARELLA and PEACHES____

The ingredients have nowhere to hide here, so do try to find buffalo mozzarella (mozzarella di bufala), for an extra-special creaminess and flavour.

SERVES 4____PREP 15 minutes

INGREDIENTS

50ml olive oil
juice of 1 lemon
salt and pepper

50g rocket leaves
2 balls of buffalo mozzarella
4 peaches, pitted and cut into wedges

METHOD

____Make a simple dressing in a small bowl by whisking together the oil and lemon juice with salt and pepper to taste.

____Scatter the rocket over a large platter. Tear the mozzarella into pieces and arrange over the rocket, with the peaches. Drizzle with the dressing.

____VIETNAMESE PRAWN and PAK CHOI SOUP____

Fresh and hot. Add more lime juice or chilli to customise your bowl.

SERVES 4____PREP 10 minutes____COOK 10 minutes

INGREDIENTS

500ml chicken stock
100g cooked prawns, shelled and deveined
1 small red chilli, finely chopped, or to taste
100ml coconut milk
100g cooked rice noodles

100g sliced pak choi
juice of 1 lime, or to taste
fish sauce, to taste (optional)
salt
50g coriander leaves, chopped

METHOD

____Bring the stock to a simmer. Add the prawns, chilli and coconut milk, cook for two minutes, then add everything else except the coriander, season and cook for two minutes.

____Remove from the heat, add the coriander and serve in large bowls.

___TOMATO EGGS___

An old recipe that makes a wonderfully comforting supper. It's gluten-free, too.

SERVES 2___PREP 5 minutes___COOK 20 minutes___ANNIE FORT

INGREDIENTS
4 tomatoes
salt and pepper
4 eggs
a little unsalted butter

METHOD
___Preheat the oven to 180°C/fan 160°C/gas mark 4.
___Cut the tops off the tomatoes and scoop out the centres with a spoon. Put the tomatoes in a small ovenproof dish and sprinkle the insides with salt and pepper.
___Crack an egg into each tomato, adding more salt and pepper if you wish. Place a small knob of butter on the tops.
___Bake in the oven for 20 minutes, or until the eggs are done to your liking, then serve.

___CHORIZO and EGGS in TOMATO SAUCE

Crowd-pleasing flavours here and a Spanish breakfast-for-supper vibe, too.

SERVES 2___PREP 5 minutes___COOK 30 minutes

INGREDIENTS
4 small chorizo sausages
olive oil
1 onion, finely chopped
2 garlic cloves,
    finely chopped
2 x 400g cans of
    chopped tomatoes
4 large eggs
8 basil leaves

METHOD
___Fry the sausages in a little olive oil, ensuring they are cooked on all sides. Remove from the pan and set aside.
___Add the onion to the pan and cook until soft, then add the garlic and stir for a minute before tipping in the tomatoes, stirring well. Mix in 200ml of water and cook until the sauce has thickened.
___Return the chorizo to the pan and crack the eggs directly into the sauce.
___Simmer until the eggs are cooked to your liking.
___Sprinkle with the torn basil and serve with crusty bread.

INGREDIENTS

100g self-raising flour

100g Parmesan, finely
  grated

50g parsley leaves, finely
  chopped

salt and pepper

4 large eggs, lightly beaten

400g skinless chicken
  breasts, chopped

vegetable oil, to deep-fry

INGREDIENTS

100ml whole milk

50g unsalted butter,
  chopped

125g plain flour

3 eggs, lightly beaten

85g Gruyère, finely grated

85g aged Parmesan,
  finely grated

salt and pepper

___PARMESAN CHICKEN POPCORN___

These are lovely with a dip on the side: try sweet chilli sauce, or a flavoured mayonnaise.

SERVES 4___PREP 15 minutes___COOK 10–15 minutes

METHOD
___Put half the flour in a bowl. Add the Parmesan, parsley, salt and pepper and eggs and beat to form a batter.
___Put the remaining flour in a broad, shallow dish and use it to coat the chicken.
___Heat the oil for deep-frying in a very large saucepan or a deep-fat fryer. If using a saucepan, the oil should come no more than one-third of the way up the sides of the pan. Heat it until it reaches 160°C (325°F); if you don't have a thermometer, a piece of bread thrown in should sizzle, but not too fiercely.
___Dip the floured chicken pieces in the batter to coat, then fry a few pieces at a time until cooked through, puffed up and golden brown, turning once with a slotted spoon. It should take about five minutes, depending on the size of the chicken pieces. Drain on kitchen paper and keep warm while you fry the remaining batches. Serve hot with salad.

___CLASSIC GOUGERES___

Familiar to all, irresistible and far easier than you might have imagined. You will need a piping bag.

MAKES 35–40___PREP 10 minutes___COOK 25 minutes___JULES HECKMAN HUGHES

METHOD
___Preheat the oven to 200°C/fan 180°C/gas mark 6.
___Put the milk, butter and 100ml of water into a saucepan and bring to a rolling boil.
___Take the pan off the heat and beat in the flour. Return it to the heat and beat until the mixture is shiny and leaves the side of the pan cleanly. Cook for one or two minutes before transferring to an electric mixer. Beat for two minutes until slightly cooled.
___Slowly add the eggs, ensuring they are fully incorporated. The mix should be smooth, shiny and fairly firm. Stir in the cheeses and season with salt and pepper.
___Pipe into small mounds on a baking tray lined with baking parchment.
___Bake for 20–25 minutes until well risen and a rich gold colour. Cool before serving.

___BANG BANG PRAWNS___

A simple cold starter. If you prefer, use raw prawns and sear them before serving with the sauce.

SERVES 4___PREP 15 minutes___COOK 10 minutes

INGREDIENTS
150ml coconut milk
100g smooth peanut butter
Thai fish sauce (optional)
lime juice (optional)
12 Baby Gem lettuce leaves
400g large cooked prawns,
   shelled and deveined
1 small red chilli, finely chopped

METHOD
___Put the coconut milk and peanut butter into a heavy-based saucepan and cook until the mix becomes a smooth sauce, then remove from the heat. Taste and stir in some fish sauce and lime juice, if you like, to taste.
___Arrange the lettuce leaves over four plates, or a large platter. Scatter the prawns over the lettuce.
___Drizzle the peanut and coconut sauce over the prawns, scatter with the red chilli and serve.

___APRICOT COUNTRY PATE___

There's no mystery to making pâté; a little light frying, then just mix everything together.

SERVES about 10___PREP 15 minutes___COOK 90 minutes___VIC LAWS

INGREDIENTS
2 onions, finely chopped
50g unsalted butter
450g pig's liver, trimmed
450g minced pork
4 garlic cloves, crushed
250g streaky bacon
8 dried apricots, chopped
chopped herb leaves, such
   as sage, to taste
mace and nutmeg, to taste
20ml brandy
2 egg whites
flavourless vegetable oil

METHOD
___Preheat the oven to 180°C/fan 160°C/gas mark 4. Sauté the onions in the butter and, when soft, put in a large bowl. In the same pan, lightly cook the liver, then roughly chop it.
___Mix the liver, pork, onions and garlic. Chop half the bacon and mix in, with the apricots, herbs, spices, brandy, egg whites, and a generous hand with the salt and pepper.
___Lightly oil ovenproof dishes or terrine tins and fill with the mix. Cover with the remaining bacon. Place in a roasting tin. Pour boiling water into the tin, to come halfway up the sides of the terrines. Bake for 90 minutes, until coming away from the tins. Leave to cool; the juices will be re-absorbed.
___Leave for about 24 hours in the fridge and serve with hot buttered toast and gherkins, or wrap and freeze until needed.

___CAULIFLOWER, WHITE BEAN and FETA SALAD___

Beautiful with its multiple shades of white, accented by the sharp bite of feta.

SERVES 6___PREP 15 minutes___COOK 1 minute___DEBBIE WHITWORTH

INGREDIENTS
6–7 tbsp olive oil
1 tsp finely chopped
   rosemary needles
2 tbsp lemon juice, plus 2½ tsp
   finely grated unwaxed lemon zest
1 tbsp red wine vinegar
salt and pepper
1 cauliflower, cut into
   small florets
400g can of white beans,
   drained and rinsed
2 white endives/chicory, finely sliced
1 tbsp finely snipped chives
2 tbsp finely chopped parsley leaves
100g feta cheese

METHOD
___Combine the oil and rosemary in a small saucepan. Stir over a medium heat just until fragrant, about one minute. Cool.

___Whisk the lemon juice and zest, vinegar, salt and pepper in a small bowl.

___Combine the cauliflower, beans, endives, chives, parsley and rosemary oil in a medium bowl and toss together gently. Add the dressing and toss to coat.

___Season the salad with salt and pepper and crumble over the feta cheese to serve.

___TOMATO, ROASTED BABY ONION and PESTO SALAD___

SERVES 4___PREP 5 minutes___COOK 25 minutes

INGREDIENTS
200g button onions, peeled
2 tbsp olive oil
100g baby spinach
200g tomatoes, sliced
50g pesto

METHOD
___Preheat the oven to 200°C/fan 180°C/gas mark 6.

___Coat the onions in the oil and roast for 25 minutes, or until just tender and slightly charred, increasing the oven temperature if necessary to achieve this.

___Arrange the spinach on a serving dish, scatter with the tomatoes and onions and drizzle with the pesto.

___TREACLE-CURED SALMON, APPLE VINAIGRETTE___

Yes there are several stages here, but none of them are difficult. And the salmon has to be marinated 48 hours ahead of serving, so it's easy to break the recipe down into manageable parts.

SERVES 12___PREP 30 minutes___COOK 10 minutes___ALBERT ROUX

INGREDIENTS

For the fish
150g black treacle
10g fennel seeds
10g coriander seeds
finely grated zest of
    1 unwaxed orange
    and 1 unwaxed lemon
20g brown sugar
60g rock salt
1.5kg side of salmon,
    trimmed and pinboned

For the vinaigrette
300ml apple cider, plus a
    little more if needed
2 egg yolks
50g Dijon mustard
200ml olive oil
200ml vegetable oil
salt and pepper

To serve
4 apples, finely chopped
1 head of celery, strings
    removed with a vegetable
    peeler, finely chopped
micro herbs (optional)

METHOD

___Gently warm the treacle to soften. Place the fennel and coriander seeds in a dry frying pan and toss over a high heat to toast the spices slightly. Place in a small food processor with the citrus zests, brown sugar, rock salt and melted treacle. Process briefly.

___While the mixture is still warm, place the salmon on a large piece of cling film, skin side down. Spread over an even, thick layer of the treacle mixture, making sure all the salmon is covered. Wrap with a few layers of cling film, keeping the marinade tightly on the fish. Leave for 24 hours in the fridge, skin side down. Turn and marinate for another 24 hours.

___After 48 hours, remove the fish from the marinade and rinse very briefly under cold running water. Dry and wrap again with cling film. Keep refrigerated.

___For the vinaigrette, boil the cider until it is syrupy, then cool. Place the egg yolks, mustard and reduced cider in a bowl and process with a hand-held blender. Add the oils gradually while the blender is running. Season to taste. If the vinaigrette is too thick, add a little cider.

___Serve the salmon thinly sliced with the apples, celery and micro herbs, if using, drizzling with the apple vinaigrette.

___ROASTED HERITAGE BEETS, ORANGE DRESSING___

Do try and get a mixture of coloured beetroots here, as it adds loads of interest to the dish.

SERVES 4___PREP 10 minutes___COOK 15 minutes

INGREDIENTS

400g baby beets, ideally
   heritage mixed colours
2 tbsp olive oil, plus 50ml
   for the dressing
salt and pepper
leaves from a sprig of thyme
juice of 2 oranges
1 tbsp wholegrain mustard

METHOD

___Preheat the oven to 180°C/fan 160°C/gas mark 4.
___Wash and trim the beets, retaining the leafy parts if they
look fresh and lovely. Halve them and coat with the 2 tbsp of
oil, salt and pepper. Place in a roasting tray with the thyme.
___Roast in the hot oven for 15 minutes, or until just cooked.
(Check with the tip of a sharp knife, the largest beet halves
should be just tender all the way through.)
___Remove from the oven and allow to cool a little.
Meanwhile, whisk the 50ml of olive oil in a small bowl with
the orange juice and mustard and season to taste.
___Cover the beets with the dressing and toss to coat. Serve.

___BABY BEETS with BURNED CARROT PUREE___

SERVES 4___PREP 10 minutes___COOK 30 minutes___JULES HECKMAN HUGHES

INGREDIENTS

10 carrots
salt and pepper
150ml extra virgin olive oil
20 baby beets
50g unsalted butter
selection of herbs and edible
   flowers (such as chervil,
   tarragon, parsley, violas,
   wild garlic flowers)

METHOD

___Preheat the grill to high. Place the carrots on a baking
tray and grill to burn the skin off. When the skin is dark,
steam the carrots until tender. Place in a blender, season,
add the oil and blend to a very smooth, dark purée.
___Wash the beetroots and trim the leaves and roots. Cook
in salted boiling water until tender. Peel and quarter them.
___Heat the butter in a pan and toss the beetroots in it.
___Spread a little carrot purée artistically on plates; it
should have a smoky flavour. Top with the beetroot pieces
and garnish with a selection of herbs and edible flowers.

___MUSHROOMS A LA GRECQUE___

Best eaten at room temperature as a starter, or as a salad with crusty French bread.

SERVES 4___PREP 10 minutes___COOK 20 minutes

INGREDIENTS
150ml dry white wine
2 ripe tomatoes, finely chopped
2 garlic cloves, finely chopped
1 tsp coriander seeds
sprig of thyme
½ small onion, finely chopped
1 bay leaf
400g button mushrooms, halved
juice of ½ lemon
3 tbsp olive oil
2 tsp chopped parsley leaves

METHOD
___Put the wine, tomatoes, garlic, coriander, thyme, onion and bay leaf in a saucepan and bring to the boil. Add the mushrooms and cover. Simmer for 15 minutes.

___Remove from the heat and add the lemon juice, olive oil and parsley, season to taste and allow to cool. Refrigerate overnight. Allow to return to room temperature to serve.

___AUBERGINE CAPONATA___

Lovely on a buffet or as a side dish to any Mediterranean-style meal.

SERVES 10___PREP 15 minutes___COOK 30 minutes___JULES HECKMAN HUGHES

INGREDIENTS
135ml olive oil
900g aubergines, finely chopped
125g onions, finely chopped
30g green olives, finely chopped
30g drained capers, finely chopped
60ml red wine or sherry vinegar
30g caster sugar, or to taste
30g sultanas
30g lightly toasted pine nuts
250g tomatoes, chopped

METHOD
___In a frying pan, heat half the oil over a medium heat until hot but not smoking, then add the aubergine and cook for 15 minutes, or until tender. Transfer to a bowl.

___Add the remaining oil to the pan and cook the onion for three minutes, then add the olives, capers, vinegar, sugar, sultanas, pine nuts and tomatoes and cook, covered, for five more minutes.

___Combine all the ingredients. Serve warm, at room temperature, or chilled. Season to taste before serving.

___CRAB SALAD___

A new take on Caesar salad, with a glorious sweet British crab as the centrepiece.

SERVES 2___PREP 15 minutes___COOK 5 minutes___JOHN RETALLICK

INGREDIENTS

1 small cooked crab,
   cleaned and dressed
15g fine white breadcrumbs
salt and white pepper
1 Cos lettuce, leaves washed
   and dried
1 thick slice of sturdy country
   bread, cut into 1cm cubes
large knob of unsalted butter

1 garlic clove
1 egg yolk
1 tsp Dijon mustard
splash of white wine
olive oil
4 anchovy fillets in oil,
   drained, but oil reserved
25g Parmesan, finely grated
small bunch of watercress

METHOD

___Separate the white and brown crab meat. Mix the brown meat with the breadcrumbs. Season both white and brown meat to taste. Break the lettuce leaves into bite-sized pieces.

___For the croutons, fry the bread cubes carefully in the butter and garlic until golden brown and crisp. Drain thoroughly. Discard the garlic clove.

___To make the dressing, put the egg yolk, mustard and white wine into a bowl and whisk, gradually adding enough olive oil (with a little anchovy oil) to make a thick Caesar salad-type dressing. Season to taste.

___Place the lettuce leaves in a serving dish, scatter with both types of crab meat and drizzle a little of the dressing over. Decorate with the anchovy fillets and garlic croutons. Finish with the grated Parmesan and a little fresh watercress.

___Serve the remaining dressing on the side.

___FETA, BLACK OLIVE and FENNEL SALAD___

This takes minutes to throw together and is lovely with warm pitta, or as a side dish with a barbecue.

SERVES 4___PREP 15 minutes

INGREDIENTS
200g feta cheese, chopped
50g black olives, pitted
150g ripe tomatoes, chopped
1 large cucumber, deseeded
  and chopped
100g fennel, thinly sliced
100ml extra virgin olive oil
juice of 1 lemon
2 tsp chopped mint leaves
salt and pepper

METHOD
___Mix the feta cheese, olives and all the vegetables together in a salad bowl.
___In a small bowl, make the dressing by whisking together the olive oil, lemon juice, mint, salt and pepper. Toss the salad with the dressing.
___Serve.

___CHICKEN NOODLE SALAD___

SERVES 4___PREP 15 minutes___COOK 25 minutes

INGREDIENTS
4 skinless chicken breasts
100ml sweet chilli sauce
50ml rice vinegar
25ml light soy sauce
juice of 1 lime, or to taste
10g brown sugar
300g cooked flat rice noodles
150g cucumber, cut into
  5cm batons
25g coriander, chopped
50g spring onions, chopped

METHOD
___Preheat the oven to 170°C/fan 150°C/gas mark 3½.
___Coat the chicken breasts with half the sweet chilli sauce and roast for 25 minutes, or until the juices run clear.
___In a bowl, mix the rice vinegar, soy sauce, lime juice and brown sugar. Taste and add more lime juice, if you like.
___Arrange the rice noodles evenly on a serving platter, then sprinkle over the cucumber, coriander and spring onion.
___Drizzle the dressing over.
___When the chicken is cooked, slice across the breasts 5cm thick and arrange over the noodles, drizzle the remaining sweet chilli sauce over and serve.

___ORZO, ROAST SQUASH and HERB SALAD___

Satisfying enough to be served as a main course and popular with children.

SERVES 4___PREP 15 minutes___COOK 30 minutes

INGREDIENTS

200g peeled and chopped
  butternut squash
50ml olive oil, plus more
  for the squash
salt and pepper
250g orzo pasta
30g mixed seasonal herb leaves
juice of 1 lemon
50g tomatoes, finely chopped

METHOD

___Preheat the oven to 180°C/fan 160°C/gas mark 4.
Place the squash in a baking tray with a little olive oil,
toss to coat, season, then roast for 30 minutes.
___Meanwhile, cook the pasta according to the packet
instructions, then drain and refresh under cold running
water. Chop the herbs. Mix the lemon juice with the
50ml of olive oil and the chopped tomatoes.
___Add the squash, herbs and tomato dressing to the
pasta and mix together. Serve in bowls.

___FENNEL and ORANGE SALAD___

The sharp, aniseed flavours here work brilliantly with grilled fish, especially a meaty red mullet.

SERVES 4 as a side dish___PREP 15 minutes___GARY GATES

INGREDIENTS

1 large onion, thinly sliced
1 fennel bulb
1 large orange
dash of lemon juice
splash of good extra virgin
  olive oil
salt and pepper
handful of pine nuts

METHOD

___Put the onion in a salad bowl.
___Trim the fennel bulb, reserving any fronds. Halve the
bulb and remove and discard the core. Thinly slice the rest
and mix in the bowl with the onion.
___Take the orange and, with a sharp knife, cut the top and
bottom off. Next, using downwards strokes, cut away the
skin and pith, then slice out the segments, cutting between
the membranes. Put the orange segments into the bowl.
___Add the lemon juice and olive oil, season lightly and mix
it all together. Scatter a few pine nuts over and, if you had
them, the fennel fronds, finely chopped. There you have it!

___PILCHARD ESCABECHE___

Get a fishmonger to pinbone the pilchards. Fashionable and, even better, it needs to be made ahead.

SERVES 6___PREP 20 minutes___COOK 15 minutes___JULES HECKMAN HUGHES

INGREDIENTS

20 spanking-fresh pilchard fillets, or even mackerel, skin on, pinbones removed
6 tbsp olive oil
1 bay leaf
leaves from 2 sprigs of thyme, or summer savory
2 tsp coriander seeds, lightly crushed
2 star anise
2 banana shallots, finely chopped
1 fennel bulb, trimmed, cored and finely sliced
1 carrot, finely sliced
2 garlic cloves, crushed
salt and pepper
2 tsp caster sugar
pinch of saffron strands
300ml white wine vinegar
80ml cider vinegar

METHOD

___Wash and dry the fish fillets and lightly score the skin. Place in a shallow, non-reactive container (not metal!), add half the oil and the herbs.

___Toast the coriander and star anise in a dry frying pan, then remove from the heat and add the remaining oil. Now add the shallots, fennel, carrot and garlic and return to a medium heat. Cook until the shallots are transparent. Season, then stir in the sugar and saffron. Add both vinegars and bring to the boil. Reduce the heat and simmer for five minutes, then remove from the heat and let it cool for another five minutes.

___Season the fish, pour over the vinegar mixture, cover and chill for at least 12 hours.

___Serve with rye toast and a watercress salad.

___EASY PEASY TART___

This lovely tart needs a bit of baking, but is a cinch to put together from storecupboard ingredients.

SERVES 6–8___PREP 20 minutes___COOK 55 minutes___HUGH MERRILL

INGREDIENTS

225g ready-made all-butter shortcrust pastry
plain flour, to dust
600g peas (frozen or fresh)
salt and pepper
3 eggs

300ml whipping cream
150g Parmesan, finely grated
handful of basil leaves
150g feta cheese, cut into 1cm cubes
1 tbsp olive oil

METHOD

___Preheat the oven to 180°C/fan 160°C/gas mark 4.

___Roll out the pastry on a lightly floured surface and use it to line a 23cm (9in) tart tin. Line the pastry with a sheet of baking parchment and weigh it down with baking beans, dried pulses, or raw rice.

___Bake the pastry case for 15 minutes.

___Meanwhile, cook the peas in salted boiling water. Frozen peas will only need to come to the boil in the pan; fresh peas will need a couple of minutes boiling, or more, depending on their age (taste to check when they are tender). Drain the peas well.

___Place half the peas in a blender and whizz them briefly.

___Put the eggs, cream and half the Parmesan in a bowl and beat until well blended.

___Add the puréed peas and remaining whole peas, torn basil leaves, feta and salt and pepper. Pour the filling into the pastry case. Sprinkle with the remaining Parmesan and add a drizzle of olive oil.

___Bake for 40 minutes, until golden and the filling has set. Leave to cool for 30 minutes before serving.

___LINGUINE with SPICY PUMPKIN SEED PESTO___

Pumpkin seeds are a staple of Mexican food. This pesto also works beautifully with chicken.

SERVES 4___PREP 15 minutes___COOK 25 minutes___THOMASINA MIERS

INGREDIENTS

1 large, very ripe tomato
3 garlic cloves, skins on
1 habanero or Scotch bonnet
   chilli
75g pumpkin seeds
1 tbsp oregano leaves
large handful of coriander
   leaves, roughly chopped
1 tsp salt
1 small shallot,
   roughly chopped
70g pecorino, finely grated,
   plus more to serve
finely grated zest and juice
   of ½ unwaxed lime
finely grated zest and juice
   of ½ unwaxed orange
120ml extra virgin olive oil
300g linguine

METHOD

___Heat a large, heavy-based frying pan over a high heat. Place the whole tomato, garlic cloves and chilli in the pan and dry-roast until blackened, blistered and soft. The tomato takes longer, so fish out the garlic and chilli as they are cooked. Slip the skins off the garlic and deseed the chilli.

___Meanwhile, toast the pumpkin seeds in another dry frying pan until they are toasted all over and start to 'pop'. Blitz with the herbs and salt in a food processor and then add the peeled tomato, garlic, chilli, shallot and 70g of pecorino. Blitz again. Finally add the citrus zests and juices and the olive oil and blitz to a pesto.

___Cook the pasta in plenty of well-salted boiling water until al dente, then drain, reserving the cooking water.

___Toss the pasta with the pesto, followed by 2–3 tbsp of the cooking water. Allow to sit for a minute or two and add a few tbsp more cooking water if needed to loosen the sauce; this stops it from becoming dry. Serve with lots of freshly grated pecorino and, if you like, a green salad.

___MEDITERRANEAN ROAST VEG with PINE NUTS___

A simple preparation that is always welcome.

SERVES 4___PREP 15 minutes___COOK 15 minutes

INGREDIENTS
200g aubergines
200g courgettes
200g mixed peppers
50ml olive oil
juice of 1 lemon
2 garlic cloves, finely chopped
salt and pepper
20g pine nuts
20g basil leaves

METHOD
___Slice the aubergines and courgettes lengthways, 5mm thick. Slice the peppers into strips.
___Mix the olive oil, lemon juice, garlic, salt and pepper in a bowl. Dip all the vegetables in this mix while you heat a griddle pan over a high heat. Cook the vegetables on the hot griddle until tender, creating charring lines.
___Meanwhile, put the pine nuts in a dry frying pan over a medium heat and stir for a minute, until they smell toasted.
___While still warm, arrange the vegetables on a serving dish and pour over the remaining dressing. Top with the basil leaves and toasted pine nuts.

___POTATO CAKES___

Apart from being utterly delicious, these are also gluten-free.

MAKES 4___PREP 15 minutes___COOK 10 minutes___ANNIE FORT

INGREDIENTS
1 egg, lightly beaten
salt and pepper
1 medium potato, grated
1 small onion, grated (optional)
25g Cheddar, grated
a little vegetable oil

METHOD
___Put the egg in a large bowl and season it. Squeeze the grated potato to remove any liquid and add to the egg with the onion and cheese. Mix it all together.
___Heat the oil in a large frying pan.
___Place about 2 tbsp of potato mix in the pan and flatten with a spoon to make a cake; this mixture should be enough for four. Cook on each side for about four minutes until golden brown. Drain on kitchen paper to blot off excess oil, then serve.

___CARAMELISED PINK ONION TARTE TATIN___

Some recipes make tartes tatin in ovenproof frying pans, but using a tart tin is easier.

SERVES 6___PREP 10–15 minutes___COOK 1 hour___JULIE PEASGOOD

INGREDIENTS
30g unsalted butter
900g red onions, cut across into 2cm (¾in) slices
2 tbsp caster sugar
salt and pepper
2 tbsp balsamic vinegar
a little olive oil
55g sun-dried tomatoes, drained of oil and roughly chopped
225g ready-made pastry, shortcrust or puff, as you prefer
plain flour, to dust

METHOD
___Melt the butter in a frying pan large enough to hold all the onion slices in a single layer, then add the onions. Sprinkle half the sugar over and season. Pour in enough cold water to just cover the onions, bring to the boil and simmer, undisturbed, for 30 minutes, or until the onions are tender and all the liquid has evaporated to leave a sticky glaze. Be careful near the end of the cooking, because the onions can burn. Carefully pour over the balsamic vinegar.

___Preheat the oven to 220°C/fan 200°C/gas mark 7. Liberally oil a large, shallow tin, 23cm (9in) in diameter, and evenly sprinkle with the remaining sugar. Scatter in the sun-dried tomatoes, then arrange the onions in the tin and season well.

___Roll out the pastry on a lightly floured surface. It should be thin and just a little larger than the pan. Arrange it over the onions, tucking in the edges.

___Bake for 20–30 minutes until golden. Turn out on to a warmed plate and serve.

___AUBERGINE PARMIGIANA___

A little effort required, but it's simple. Err on the side of generosity with the cheeses.

SERVES 6___PREP 25 minutes___COOK 40 minutes___SADIQ KHAN

INGREDIENTS

4 aubergines
plain flour
salt and pepper
vegetable oil
500g jarred or home-made
    tomato and basil sauce
4 balls of mozzarella, sliced
2 handfuls of finely grated
    Parmesan

METHOD

___Preheat the oven to 150°C/fan 130°C/gas mark 2.
___Slice the aubergines 5mm thick. Mix some flour with salt and pepper and place in a dish. Coat the aubergine in the flour, then fry in hot vegetable oil until tender.
___Spread a little tomato sauce in a baking dish. Add a layer of aubergine, then of mozzarella, then sprinkle with Parmesan. Season well. Repeat until you have used all the ingredients, finishing with top layers of sauce, mozzarella and Parmesan, in that order, seasoning very well as you go.
___Bake for 35 minutes. Stand for 10 minutes, then serve.

___SPINACH and POTATO CAKES with TOMATO SALSA___

The salsa gives a piquant edge to these comforting potato cakes.

SERVES 4___PREP 10 minutes___COOK 10 minutes

INGREDIENTS

1 small onion, finely chopped
4 tomatoes, finely chopped
2 tsp white wine vinegar
10g parsley leaves, chopped
400g mashed potato
4 egg yolks
30g baby spinach
50g Cheddar, finely grated
50g plain flour
2 tbsp olive oil

METHOD

___Put the onion in a bowl with the tomatoes, vinegar and parsley, season well and stir.
___Mix the potato, egg yolks, spinach and cheese. Season well. Shape into 2cm-thick, 8cm-diameter rounds.
___Coat in seasoned flour (as above) and fry in hot oil on both sides until golden.
___Serve the hot potato cakes with the salsa on top.

___SPAGHETTI with GARLIC, OIL and CHILLI___

The original storecupboard supper, this is sure to become a favourite in your household.

SERVES 2___PREP 5 minutes___COOK 10 minutes___ANTONIO CARLUCCIO

INGREDIENTS
salt
180g spaghetti
6 tbsp olive oil
2 garlic cloves,
    finely chopped
1 small red chilli,
    finely chopped
a few basil leaves
    (optional)

METHOD

___Put plenty of water in a saucepan, add salt, bring to the boil, then throw in the pasta. Stir. Cook for five to six minutes until nearly done.

___Now heat the olive oil gently in a deep frying pan. Add the garlic and chilli and fry for a few seconds, or until the garlic starts to change colour; take care not to burn the garlic.

___The pasta will be ready and al dente in those few minutes. Drain it well, reserving a little of the cooking water, and put in the pan with the sauce, adding a little salt and perhaps 1–2 tbsp of the pasta cooking water. Stir a couple of times and serve, scattered with basil, if you like.

___CONCHIGLIE con PISELLE___

Far more sophisticated than the sum of its parts.

SERVES 8___PREP 5 minutes___COOK 10 minutes___DEBBIE WHITWORTH

INGREDIENTS
salt and pepper
450g conchiglie pasta
300ml double cream
450g frozen peas
finely grated pecorino,
    to taste, plus more to serve
a few mint and parsley leaves,
    roughly chopped

METHOD

___Bring a large saucepan of salted water to the boil, add the pasta and cook according to the packet instructions. When cooked, drain, reserving a little of the cooking water. Return the pasta to the cooking pot.

___Meanwhile, in another pan, bring the cream to a simmer, add the peas and cook for two minutes. Add the pecorino and cook until thickened, another minute.

___Pour the sauce over the pasta, adding some of the reserved cooking water if the pasta is dry. Season to taste.

___Sprinkle with the herbs and serve with extra cheese.

___POMEGRANATE, MINT and RED ONION COUSCOUS___

This makes a lovely side dish to eat with simply grilled chicken, or a Middle Eastern lamb tagine.

SERVES 4___PREP 20 minutes

INGREDIENTS

500ml boiling vegetable stock
200g couscous
1 pomegranate
1 small red onion,
   finely chopped
leaves from a 30g bunch
   of mint, finely chopped
50ml olive oil
juice of 1 lemon
salt and pepper

METHOD

___Pour the boiling stock over the couscous in a heatproof bowl, cover with cling film and leave to absorb the stock.
___Cut the pomegranate in half and tap out the seeds. Mix the pomegranate seeds in a bowl with all the other ingredients except the couscous.
___Add the pomegranate mixture to the couscous, mix gently and taste, being generous with the seasoning. Serve warm or cold.

___CANNELLINI BEANS with TOMATO and SAGE___

Lovely with pork. Mix the recipe up; use smoked paprika and maple syrup for a sweet, smoky bowlful.

SERVES 6___PREP 10 minutes___COOK 30 minutes___TIM WATES

INGREDIENTS

1 tbsp olive oil
1 onion, finely chopped
1 garlic clove, finely chopped
leaves from ½ bunch of sage
chilli flakes, to taste
squeeze of tomato purée
3 large tomatoes, chopped
400g can of chopped tomatoes
2 x 400g cans of cannellini
   beans, drained and rinsed

METHOD

___Preheat the oven to 180°C/fan 160°C/gas mark 4.
___Heat the oil in a large ovenproof pan and add the onion and garlic. Cook until lightly browned. Add the sage, chilli, tomato purée and both types of tomatoes and stir together well.
___Stir in the beans, mix in a little water if they seem dry, then transfer to the oven and bake, uncovered, for 20 minutes, checking halfway through that they are not dry and stirring in a little more boiling water from a kettle if they are. Serve.

___EGGS POACHED in RED WINE___

A pleasing dish, especially with a salad of lamb's lettuce. Chic and typically Burgundian.

SERVES 4___PREP 20 minutes___COOK 35 minutes___ALBERT ROUX

INGREDIENTS

1 bottle of Pinot Noir

8 eggs

60g unsalted butter, plus 60g
    clarified unsalted butter
    (see method, right)

20g plain flour

1 bouquet garni

6 crushed peppercorns

salt and pepper

4 round pieces of coarse
    white bread

1 tbsp groundnut oil, plus
    more for the lardons

12 baby onions, peeled

pinch of sugar

100g bacon lardons

2 tbsp chopped parsley leaves

METHOD

___Bring the wine to the boil in a sauté pan. Crack each egg into a cup and carefully drop it into the wine. Poach the eggs, then carefully lift them out with a slotted spoon and drain on kitchen paper. Trim off the straggly edges, cover with a damp cloth and keep at room temperature. Strain the wine through a sieve.

___In a saucepan, heat 30g of the butter, stir in the flour and cook gently for two minutes. Take the pan off the heat and gradually add the wine in which you poached the eggs, whisking all the time. Still whisking, return the pan to a low heat and bring to the boil. Add the bouquet garni and crushed peppercorns and simmer for 30 minutes.

___Take the pan off the heat and pass the sauce through a sieve, then gradually whisk in the remaining 30g of butter. Season to taste and keep warm.

___To clarify butter, heat it gently in a small saucepan. When the foaming stops, skim off any foam and pour it slowly into a dish, stopping before the milky solids at the bottom (throw these away). Heat it in a frying pan and fry the bread until golden on both sides. Place on a wire rack.

___Meanwhile, heat the oil in a frying pan, then add the onions with the pinch of sugar and some salt. Fry until caramelised. Add a little water, cover and cook gently for 15 minutes until glazed. Separately sauté the lardons with a little more oil until golden, then drain the excess fat.

___Place two eggs on each crouton and set in the centre of each plate. Heat up the sauce, adding the baby onions and lardons, and pour it generously over the top and around, sprinkle with parsley and serve.

___REGINETTE ALLA NORMA___

This is slightly more involved, but easy to make while talking to guests. And they'll want the recipe.

SERVES 4___PREP 20 minutes___COOK 40 minutes___GIORGIO LOCATELLI

INGREDIENTS

3 aubergines (preferably the
  round, pale violet ones)
salt and pepper
3 garlic cloves
sprig of rosemary
500ml vegetable oil
2 tbsp olive oil
2 tbsp tomato purée

400g reginette or mafaldine
  pasta
5 plum tomatoes, peeled
  (see page 12) and deseeded
leaves from a bunch of basil
3 tbsp salted ricotta, chopped
extra virgin olive oil, to serve

METHOD

___Preheat the oven to 220°C/fan 200°C/gas mark 7. Cut two aubergines into 3cm dice and sprinkle with salt. Cut the last aubergine in half lengthways, then put skin sides down on a work surface and score deeply in a diamond pattern. Slice one garlic clove finely and push it into the score lines with the rosemary. Put the halves back together, wrap in foil and cook for 20–25 minutes, until soft. Discard the garlic and rosemary, scoop out the flesh and put it into a colander. Leave to drain and cool, then chop finely.

___Heat the vegetable oil in a deep pan. It should be 180°C (350°F). If you don't have a thermometer, put in a few breadcrumbs, and if they sizzle straight away it is ready.

___Gently squeeze the diced aubergines to get rid of excess liquid, put them into the oil and fry them until golden, a handful at a time. Drain on kitchen paper, then pat dry.

___Finely chop the remaining two garlic cloves. Heat the olive oil in a pan large enough to take the pasta later, then add the chopped garlic and cook gently without colouring. Add the finely chopped aubergine flesh from the colander, cook gently for a couple of minutes, then add the tomato purée, stir, cook for another minute or so, then season.

___Meanwhile, bring a pan of water to the boil, add salt and put in the pasta. Cook for about a minute less than the time given on the packet, so that it is al dente. Drain, reserving some of the cooking water, and add to the sauce, with the tomatoes. Toss all together for a minute or so, then add the fried aubergines and basil. Toss again with a small amount of the salted ricotta, adding a little of the cooking water if necessary.

___Serve scattered with the rest of the salted ricotta, drizzled with extra virgin olive oil.

FISH

___PRAWN TACOS with SALSA___

Fresh flavours and quite a few of your five-a-day! Children love assembling these tacos.

SERVES 4___PREP 20 minutes___COOK 2–3 minutes___MATT TEBBUTT

INGREDIENTS

For the prawns and assembly
20 raw tiger prawns, shelled
  and deveined
1 tbsp olive oil
pinch of chilli powder
pinch of hot smoked paprika
  or cayenne pepper
8 tortillas
½ Iceberg lettuce, shredded
lime wedges, to serve

For the salsa
6 very ripe tomatoes,
  deseeded and chopped
1 ripe avocado, chopped
½ red onion, finely chopped
1 red chilli, finely chopped,
  or a few slices of
  pickled jalapeños
1 tbsp chopped coriander,
  stalks and all
2 garlic cloves, crushed
splash of sherry vinegar
2 tbsp olive oil
salt and pepper

For the sour cream
200g sour cream
juice of 2 limes
1 tbsp Tabasco sauce

METHOD

___Start by marinating the prawns in the olive oil, chilli powder and paprika. Toss together and leave while you get on with everything else.

___Make the salsa by mixing all the ingredients, then taste and season. Set aside at room temperature for the flavours to develop.

___Mix the sour cream with the lime juice and Tabasco, add a little salt and set aside.

___Heat a chargrill pan over a high heat until it is very hot, season the prawns, throw on the pan and cook for around one minute on each side until they have changed colour from blue to pink. Remove. Briefly warm the tortillas in a dry frying pan over a medium heat.

___Spoon some salsa into each tortilla, add a few prawns, a little shredded lettuce and finally the sour cream. Put some lime wedges on the side. Done!

___GRILLED TUNA, LENTILS and CAPER DRESSING___

Simple, satisfying, healthy and refreshing.

SERVES 2___PREP 15 minutes___COOK 25 minutes___MATT TEBBUTT

INGREDIENTS

For the lentils

100g Puy lentils

1 small onion, finely chopped

3 celery sticks, finely chopped

1 garlic clove, finely chopped

1 bay leaf

1–2 sprigs of thyme

salt and pepper

2 tbsp olive oil

For the tuna and dressing

100g Greek or natural yogurt

bunch of dill, finely chopped

1 tbsp olive oil, plus more
   for the tuna

squeeze of lemon juice

2 tsp small capers, drained
   and rinsed

2 × 200g tuna steaks

METHOD

___First, cook the lentils by placing them, the chopped vegetables, garlic and herbs in a pan and covering with cold water. Bring to the boil, then reduce the heat and cook for around 20 minutes, until al dente. Season with salt after cooking, drain off any excess liquid, remove the bay leaf and thyme stalks and stir in the olive oil. Taste for seasoning – lentils can take a lot of seasoning – and keep warm.

___Mix the yogurt with the dill, olive oil, lemon juice, seasoning and capers.

___When ready to serve, heat a frying pan or chargrill pan over a high heat. Season and lightly oil the tuna. When the pan is very hot, sear the tuna for no longer than one minute on each side, turning halfway through. Remove immediately and slice through each steak at an angle.

___Now pile some lentils on each plate, top with the tuna and spoon over the dressing. Serve with a simple green salad or a big plate of sliced and dressed ripe tomatoes.

_____SIMPLE FISH SOUP_____

Using a few well-chosen bought items really speeds dinner along. This is a truly luxurious plateful.

SERVES 4___PREP 10 minutes___COOK 20 minutes___ANTONIO CARLUCCIO

INGREDIENTS

6 tbsp olive oil
1 small onion, finely chopped
2–3 tbsp tomato passata
1kg mussels, cleaned
300g monkfish, cut into cubes
300g squid, cleaned and
  cut into rings
500ml good French *soupe
  de poissons* (from most
  supermarkets or delicatessens)
4 thick slices of coarse-textured
  bread

METHOD

___Heat the oil in a large saucepan and fry the onion until softened, six or seven minutes. Add the passata, bring to the boil, then reduce the heat to a simmer.

___Add the mussels, monkfish and squid rings and cook at a simmer for about 10 minutes, until the fish are cooked through and the mussels are open. Discard any mussels that haven't opened after this time.

___Stir in the fish soup and heat through gently for about five minutes, while you toast the bread.

___Place a slice of toasted bread in the bottom of each of four warmed bowls (or just serve it alongside), pour in the soup and serve.

_____PAN-FRIED PRAWNS in their SHELLS_____

A great light meal in minutes. You must have spanking fresh prawns, as they are the star here.

SERVES 4___PREP 5 minutes___COOK 5 minutes___JANE SANDERSON

INGREDIENTS

2 tbsp extra virgin olive oil
32 large raw prawns in their
  shells
4 garlic cloves,
  finely chopped
120ml dry white vermouth
3 tbsp tomato passata
salt and pepper
chopped parsley leaves

METHOD

___Heat the oil in a heavy-based frying pan over a medium heat, then add the prawns and toss. Sprinkle the garlic over the prawns and toss again.

___Add the vermouth and let it bubble, tossing the prawns until they have turned pink and cooked evenly. Add the passata, salt and pepper and stir until the prawns are coated.

___Sprinkle with parsley. Serve at once with crusty bread.

____ROAST COD with a PEA and MINT CRUST____

As easy as turning on the food processor, a dish you can prepare in advance, effortlessly.

SERVES 4___PREP 20 minutes___COOK 20 minutes

INGREDIENTS

100g frozen peas, defrosted
100g unsalted butter
juice and finely grated zest
   of 1 unwaxed lemon
leaves from 30g bunch each of
   mint and parsley, chopped
100g fresh breadcrumbs
4 x 100g portions of cod loin
100g new potatoes

METHOD

____In a food processor blend the peas, 75g of the butter, the lemon zest and mint. Scrape out into a bowl and mix with the breadcrumbs. Clean out the food processor.

____Now blend the remaining 25g of butter with the lemon juice and parsley. Chill.

____Coat the cod with the pea mixture and set aside for 30 minutes. Preheat the oven to 200°C/fan 180°C/gas mark 6.

____Bake the cod for 20 minutes, while you steam the new potatoes until tender. Coat the potatoes with the lemon and parsley butter and serve with the cod.

_____COD and CHORIZO____

A fast and furious, taste-packed supper. Drain off some of the oil if a lot comes out of the chorizo.

SERVES 4___PREP 10 minutes___COOK 20 minutes___DEBBIE WHITWORTH

INGREDIENTS

600g potatoes, cut into
   1cm cubes
110g chorizo, skinned
   and chopped
4 skinless cod fillets
1 tsp paprika
2 tbsp olive oil (if needed)
chopped parsley leaves and
   lemon wedges, to serve

METHOD

____Preheat the oven to 200°C/fan 180°C/gas mark 6. Cook the potatoes in boiling water for three minutes. Drain.

____Heat a large frying pan over a medium-high heat, add the chorizo and cook for two minutes, until the oil is released, then remove from the pan.

____Dust the cod with the paprika and add to the chorizo oil in the pan. Cook for one minute on each side, until golden. Transfer to a roasting dish and bake for 10 minutes.

____Meanwhile, add olive oil to the frying pan if needed and cook the potatoes until crisp, then return the chorizo and sprinkle with parsley. Serve with the cod and lemon wedges.

_____SALMON en CROUTE_____

Ring the changes with this, adding plain cream cheese, or capers, or finely grated lemon zest.

SERVES 4___PREP 10 minutes___COOK 25 minutes

INGREDIENTS

1 ready-rolled puff pastry
   sheet
100g garlic and herb cream
   cheese
4 x 100g skinless salmon
   fillets
100g baby spinach
1 egg, lightly beaten

METHOD

___Cut the pastry sheet into four equal rectangles.

___Spread the cream cheese over each salmon fillet and cover with spinach leaves. Place each on to a piece of pastry.

___Brush the beaten egg all around the edge of the pastry sheets and fold the pastry over the salmon to form a parcel. Repeat to make four. Line a baking tray with baking parchment and place the parcels, seam sides down, on that.

___Brush with beaten egg and chill for 20 minutes or up to one day. Preheat the oven to 200°C/fan 180°C/gas mark 6.

___Slash each parcel diagonally a couple of times, then bake for 25 minutes, until golden brown and cooked through.

_____SEARED SALMON with SESAME and LIME_____

Dinner in moments. Add finely chopped chilli if you'd like a bit of heat.

SERVES 4___PREP 5 minutes___COOK 5 minutes

INGREDIENTS

4 x 100g skin-on salmon
   supremes
a little olive oil
50ml soy sauce
50ml toasted sesame oil
finely grated zest and juice
   of up to 1–1½ unwaxed
   limes, or to taste

METHOD

___Place the salmon fillets skin side down into a hot frying pan coated with the olive oil and cook until the skin is crispy. Turn over and cook for 30 more seconds, then turn out, skin side up, on to a serving dish.

___Put the soy, sesame oil and half of the lime zest and juice into a blender and whizz to emulsify. Taste and adjust the level of lime to your liking. Coat the salmon with the dressing and serve.

SALMON WRAPPED in PROSCIUTTO and PESTO

Everyone loves the flavours in this crowd-pleaser, and it's easy to scale up for larger numbers.

SERVES 2___PREP 10 minutes___COOK 10 minutes___FINLAY SCOTT

INGREDIENTS

8 slices of prosciutto
2 tsp pesto
2 salmon fillets
salt and pepper
1 celery stick, finely chopped
1 carrot, finely chopped
olive oil
400g packet or can of cooked
    Puy lentils
handful of Sun-Blush
    tomatoes, chopped
handful of herb leaves:
    parsley, thyme, rosemary
    and so on, finely chopped
100g bag of spinach leaves
lemon wedges, to serve

METHOD

___Preheat the oven to 220°C/fan 200°C/gas mark 7. Lay out four overlapping slices of prosciutto. Spread with 1 tsp of the pesto. Place a salmon fillet on top, season and seal in the prosciutto, wrapping firmly. Repeat with the remaining prosciutto, pesto and salmon.

___Line a baking tray with baking parchment and place the parcels on that, seam sides down. Roast in the hot oven for seven or eight minutes, or until cooked through, depending on the size of the fillets.

___Meanwhile, fry the celery and carrot in a little olive oil until soft. Drain the lentils and add them to the pan with the tomatoes, herbs and spinach. Cook for a few minutes, stirring, until the spinach wilts, then remove from the heat.

___Put a bed of lentils on each of two plates. Place a salmon parcel on top and drizzle restrainedly with good olive oil. Serve with lemon wedges.

____ASIAN QUICK-FRIED SQUID____

A domestic version of salt-and-pepper squid that will disappear almost as fast as it is made.

SERVES 4___PREP 20 minutes___COOK 10 minutes

INGREDIENTS

vegetable oil, to deep-fry
100g plain flour
100g cornflour
salt and pepper
400g squid, cleaned and
   cut into rings
bunch of spring onions,
   finely sliced
1 large green chilli,
   finely sliced
lime wedges, to serve

METHOD

____Heat a 5cm depth of vegetable oil in a large saucepan or a deep-fat fryer. If using a saucepan, the oil should come no more than one-third of the way up the sides of the pan. Heat it and test the temperature by dropping a cube of bread in; it should sizzle and become crispy in two minutes.

____Mix both flours together and season with salt and plenty of black pepper; be very generous indeed with the seasoning.

____Coat the squid in the flour and fry in batches so as not to crowd the pan, turning with a slotted spoon until golden all over. Remove and place on kitchen paper to soak up the oil.

____Place the squid in a large serving dish and sprinkle with the spring onions and chilli. Serve with lime wedges.

____SQUID INK TUNA PASTA____

Strong flavours update this variant of puttanesca sauce, while the dramatic appearance is thrilling.

SERVES 4___PREP 5 minutes___COOK 10 minutes___CHRISTOPHER MOORE

INGREDIENTS

1 green pepper, chopped
1 onion, finely chopped
1 garlic clove, crushed
1 tsp chilli powder
olive oil
160g can of tuna, drained
400g can chopped tomatoes
230g jar of pitted black olives
500g squid ink linguine

METHOD

____Fry the green pepper, onion, garlic and chilli powder in oil for four or five minutes, until softened. Add the tuna, chopped tomatoes, olives and seasoning and simmer. Don't stir it too much, as it's nice if the tuna stays in large flakes.

____Meanwhile, place the pasta in boiling water and cook according to the packet instructions, then drain and add to the tuna sauce, with a very little of the cooking water if it seems a little dry. Return to the heat briefly to amalgamate the flavours, then serve.

TUNA STEAK with CAPERS, OLIVES and TOMATO

Sophisticated and light, smart enough to serve to friends and quick enough to do so on a weeknight.

SERVES 4___PREP 10 minutes___COOK 10 minutes

INGREDIENTS

500g ripe tomatoes, chopped
olive oil
2 garlic cloves, finely chopped
50g capers, drained
   and rinsed
50g pitted black olives
10 basil leaves, torn
4 x 200g tuna steaks
salt and pepper

METHOD

___Gently fry the tomatoes in a generous amount of olive oil in a large frying pan. When soft, add the garlic and cook for a further two minutes. Add the capers, olives and torn basil leaves, mix well and set aside, keeping warm.

___Add a little more olive oil to a large hot frying pan (or use a griddle pan and oil the fish, not the pan) and sear the tuna steaks, ensuring the outside is charred but keeping the middle pink. Pour over the sauce, season to taste and serve hot, with green salad.

ROAST FISH with PEPPERS

A simple and colourful dish with sweet flavours that children will love.

SERVES 4___PREP 10 minutes___COOK 15 minutes

INGREDIENTS
olive oil
1 large red pepper, deseeded
   and sliced
1 large green pepper,
   deseeded and sliced
1 large yellow pepper,
   deseeded and sliced
2 garlic cloves, finely sliced
4 x 200g cod or hake fillets
salt and pepper
juice of 1 lemon

METHOD
___Preheat the oven to 180°C/fan 160°C/gas mark 4.

___Heat a little olive oil in a large frying pan and add the peppers. Cook until they soften, then add the garlic and continue to cook gently, but do not allow the garlic to brown or it will become bitter.

___Meanwhile, brush the fish with olive oil, season with salt and pepper and roast for 10 minutes, until cooked through.

___Remove the peppers from the pan, squeeze over the lemon juice and mix it in. Serve the fish with the peppers and their juices poured over.

MEAT

___COQ A LA BIERE___

The original version of this was made with cockerel (coq), but this recipe uses free-range chicken.

SERVES 4___PREP 5 minutes___COOK 1 hour___ALBERT ROUX

INGREDIENTS
1 free-range, preferably organic, chicken (about 1.5kg)
olive oil
unsalted butter
50g shallots, finely chopped
200g button mushrooms, sliced
1½ tbsp brandy
330ml bottle of beer, preferably bitter
1 tsp brown sugar
200ml double cream
salt and pepper

METHOD
___Preheat the oven to 220°C/fan 200°C/gas mark 7.

___Put the chicken on its side in an enamelled cast-iron pan with a little olive oil and butter and roast for about 40 minutes; baste the bird several times during the cooking, turning it on to its other side and finally on to its back, breast upwards. When cooked, transfer the chicken on to a plate, breast down so that the juices permeate the meat while it rests. (To test if it is cooked, insert a sharp knife between the thigh and the body, in the thickest part of the bird. The juices that emerge should run clear. If there is any trace of pink, cook for a few minutes more, then test again.)

___Discard the fat from the roasting pan and add a knob of fresh butter, place over a low heat and sweat the shallots until translucent, stirring with a wooden spoon. Add the mushrooms and cook for a further three minutes. Pour in the brandy and scrape the pan with the spoon to deglaze fully. When the pan is almost dry, pour in the beer and sugar, bring to the boil, then reduce it by half. Add the cream and reduce again to a light sauce consistency.

___Whisk in 50g butter, cut into small pieces, to give the sauce sheen, and season to taste with salt and pepper.

___Carve the chicken and serve with the hot beer and mushroom sauce.

___SILVANO'S STEAK TARTARE___

This can be put together in front of your guests at the table, if you prepare the ingredients first.

SERVES 4___PREP 15 minutes___SILVANO GIRALDIN

INGREDIENTS

1kg good-quality rump or sirloin steak
2 egg yolks
1 tbsp Dijon mustard
2 tbsp tomato ketchup
3 tbsp finely chopped onions
2 tbsp chopped rinsed capers
salt and pepper
a few drops of Tabasco sauce
1 tbsp Worcestershire sauce
3½ tbsp very good-quality olive oil

METHOD

___Use a very sharp knife to mince the beef. This way it gets a better texture than if you use a machine.

___In a bowl, mix all the other ingredients with a whisk, adding the olive oil at the end and whisking to emulsify. Add the beef and mix it again very well, this time with a fork.

___Divide the mixture into four and shape each piece into a round, or spoon into a ramekin.

___Serve with hot sourdough toast and chips.

___SEARED BEEF with TERIYAKI SAUCE___

An exciting, different way to serve steak. Add steamed jasmine rice or noodles and stir-fried greens.

SERVES 4___PREP 5 minutes___COOK 10 minutes___KEVIN MCGRATH

INGREDIENTS
a little flavourless vegetable
  oil
50ml soy sauce
75ml mirin
25g brown sugar
4 × 100g fillet steaks

METHOD
___Heat a heavy-based frying pan and add a little oil. Mix the soy, mirin and sugar in a bowl.

___Sear the steaks in the pan on one side, then flip over and sear the other side. Now add some of the teriyaki sauce to the pan and bring to the boil. Simmer until thick.

___Remove the steaks from the pan when they are done to your liking, and allow to rest.

___Add the remaining sauce to the pan and boil until it, too, is thick.

___Slice the beef thinly and drizzle over the thickened sauce. Serve.

___SPICED BEEF with NOODLE and CUCUMBER SALAD___

A satisfying near-instant supper, with the fresh flavours of mint and smoked paprika adding interest.

SERVES 2___PREP 15 minutes___COOK 5–10 minutes___MATT TEBBUTT

INGREDIENTS

100g thick or medium
  rice noodles
olive oil
salt and pepper
2 × 200g sirloin steaks
1 red pepper, deseeded
  and sliced
1 green pepper, deseeded
  and sliced
½ red onion, finely sliced
½ cucumber, deseeded and
  finely sliced
2 garlic cloves, finely chopped
6–8 tbsp oloroso sherry
1 tbsp very finely chopped
  thyme leaves
leaves from a small bunch of
  mint, finely chopped
shake or 2 of smoked paprika

METHOD

___First, soak the noodles for a few minutes in boiling water, until soft. Drain, flick with a little olive oil and set aside in a large serving dish.

___Heat a frying pan until fiercely hot, then season and oil the steaks and sear them hard on both sides to set a really good colour, but leaving the beef perfectly rare on the inside... this should take no more than a few minutes in total. Remove and rest.

___Now throw the peppers, onion, cucumber and garlic in the pan and sauté for a few minutes to soften. Add the sherry and a glug of olive oil, swirl around the pan for a minute to boil off the alcohol, then tip over the noodles.

___Cut the rested beef into thickish slices and toss these, too, with the noodles and vegetables, adding the herbs, smoked paprika, salt to taste, and any of the juices that came out of the meat.

___Serve.

___JERK CHICKEN with TOMATO SAUCE___

If you know your guests are up for it, chop the scotch bonnet chilli, though make very sure first!

SERVES 4___PREP 15 minutes___COOK 40 minutes___WILLIAM ATKINSON

INGREDIENTS
4 chicken legs (drumsticks and thighs together)
50g jerk seasoning
vegetable oil
2 x 400g cans of chopped tomatoes
sprig of thyme
2 garlic cloves, finely chopped
2.5cm root ginger, finely chopped or grated
1 scotch bonnet chilli
juice of 1 lemon, plus lemon wedges to serve
bunch of spring onions, finely chopped
1 tsp caster sugar

METHOD
___Coat the chicken legs with half the jerk seasoning and fry in a little hot oil on both sides until well browned.

___Add the tomatoes, thyme, garlic, ginger, remaining jerk seasoning and 100ml of water and simmer for 20 minutes.

___Add the whole scotch bonnet chilli (or chop it if you prefer, see recipe introduction), lemon juice, spring onions and sugar and simmer for a further 20 minutes, or until the chicken legs are cooked. Remove and discard the chilli, if you left it whole.

___Serve the chicken and sauce with boiled rice and lemon wedges.

___THAI-STYLE PORK CHOPS___

SERVES 4___PREP 15 minutes___COOK 30 minutes___SALLY SCOTT

INGREDIENTS

For the pork

4 large pork chops, or pork steaks

vegetable oil

2–3 tbsp red Thai curry paste

100g jasmine rice

50g coriander leaves, chopped

50g Thai basil leaves, shredded

bunch of spring onions, finely chopped

lime wedges, to serve

For the dressing

50ml fish sauce

50ml light soy sauce

juice of 1 lime

30g soft brown sugar

$\frac{1}{2}$ tsp cayenne pepper

METHOD

___Preheat the oven to 160°C/fan 140°C/gas mark 3.

___Fry the pork chops in a little hot oil on both sides for one minute on each side. Remove from the pan into a roasting tin and coat with the curry paste, then bake for 25 minutes, or until cooked through. (Or you can choose to finish cooking them in the pan for more colour, if you prefer.)

___Meanwhile, cook the rice in plenty of boiling water until just cooked, then drain, mix in the coriander and cover to keep warm.

___For the dressing, mix all the ingredients in a small bowl until the sugar dissolves.

___Remove the chops from the oven and carve each into six or seven slices.

___Divide the rice between four plates, arrange the pork on top, sprinkle with the Thai basil and spring onions and finish with the dressing. Serve with lime wedges.

___COTE DE BOEUF BORDELAISE___

A fancy dish for a fancy occasion, this is suitable for the grandest guest. Quite delicious.

SERVES 4___PREP 20 minutes___COOK 1 hour___ALBERT ROUX

INGREDIENTS
60g unsalted butter
60g finely chopped shallots
200ml red Bordeaux wine
1 bouquet garni
1 tsp peppercorns
200ml veal stock
salt and pepper
a little chicken stock (optional)
400g bone marrow (optional, order from your butcher)
2 x 500g ribeye steaks, bone in (order from your butcher)
1 tbsp groundnut oil
1 tbsp finely chopped parsley

METHOD
___Melt half the butter in a frying pan and sweat the shallots until tender but with no colour. Add the red wine, bouquet garni and peppercorns and boil to reduce by half. Add the veal stock. Return to the boil, then reduce the heat and simmer for 20 minutes. Remove from the heat and discard the bouquet garni.
___Strain the sauce, return to the cleaned pan and bring back to a simmer. Chop the remaining butter. Whisk the butter cube by cube into the sauce, whisking well after each addition. Season to taste.
___Meanwhile, to cook the bone marrow, if using, bring the chicken stock to a steady simmer. Add the bone marrow and return to a simmer. Cook for about 15 minutes, or until the marrow is hot in the centre. Cut into slices and chill.
___Cook the steaks in the groundnut oil in a hot frying or griddle pan to your liking, then allow them to rest.
___Reheat the marrow in the hot sauce, slice the steak and pour over the sauce and marrow. Sprinkle with parsley.
___For a delectable accompaniment, serve with sautéed porcini with garlic and parsley.

___CARPET BAG STEAK with HORSERADISH BUTTER___

Good for a special, comforting winter feast. Serve with good claret; what more could you want?

SERVES 4___PREP 15 minutes___COOK 15 minutes___JOHN RETALLICK

INGREDIENTS
250g unsalted butter, softened, plus more for the sauce
1 tsp double cream
50–60g horseradish root, grated
cayenne pepper
2 × 285g (5cm-thick) aged sirloin steaks
Worcestershire sauce
salt and pepper
6 oysters, shelled (native if possible)
a little rapeseed oil
handful of chervil leaves, finely chopped

METHOD
___Make the butter. Put the butter in a bowl and beat it with the cream, horseradish and cayenne. Make it into a log, then wrap in cling film and chill to harden.

___Take a steak and make a slit or pocket in the non-fat side. Sprinkle it inside with Worcestershire sauce, salt and pepper. Place three oysters into the pocket and seal with cocktail sticks. Repeat to flavour and stuff the second steak.

___Heat a little oil in a large frying pan, allowing it to get really hot.

___Put the steaks in the pan, season with a little sea salt and pepper, and cook until caramelised on one side. Turn over and repeat. Be careful not to burn the juices; as the steak cooks, pour them off and keep to one side. The steak should be cooked to your preference, but ideally served medium-rare. Remove from the pan and allow to rest for five minutes. Remove the cocktail sticks and cut each in half to serve.

___Return the juices to the pan and heat, whisking in a few knobs of butter to thicken. Sprinkle with the chervil and serve this sauce with the steaks, melting discs of the horseradish butter over each piece.

___You will have more horseradish butter than you need, but it freezes well, wrapped in cling film and then in foil.

PUDDINGS

___CAKES IN MUGS___

How quickly this cooks depends on the microwave… that's a good excuse to try it a few times!

MAKES 1___PREP 10 minutes___COOK 2 minutes___DEBBIE WHITWORTH

INGREDIENTS

For a chocolate cake
4 tbsp self-raising flour
4 tbsp caster sugar
pinch of salt
2 tbsp cocoa powder
1 egg, lightly beaten
3 tbsp milk
few drops of vanilla or other extract
　　(orange, peppermint and so on)
3 tbsp vegetable oil
2 tbsp chocolate chips/nuts/raisins
　　and so on (optional)

For a vanilla cake
65g plain flour
2 tbsp granulated sugar
pinch of salt
1 egg, lightly beaten
100ml milk
1 tbsp vanilla extract
2 tbsp unsalted butter, melted

METHOD

___Use the largest microwaveable mug that you have, to avoid it overflowing in the oven.

___Add the flour, sugar and salt – and cocoa if using – and mix. Add the egg and mix it in a bit. Don't worry if there's still some dry mix in the mug. In another bowl or cup, whisk together the milk and vanilla extract, or other extract, with the oil or melted butter.

___Make a well, as far as you can, in the centre of the dry ingredients and pour in the milk mixture. Mix as well as you are able until the batter is smooth and well combined. Add the chocolate chips, nuts or raisins, if using, and mix again.

___Centre the mug in the middle of the microwave plate and microwave on the high setting for 90 seconds to two minutes. (This depends on your microwave, test after the shorter time period and check if it is firm to the touch; if not, continue to microwave until it is.) When it is firm to the touch, eat and enjoy!

___Next time, try it with peanut butter, or chocolate-hazelnut spread, or...

___WARM CITRUS SALAD with GRANOLA___

Equally at home as a pudding or breakfast. The tart flavours really wake up the palate.

SERVES 4___PREP 10 minutes___COOK 2 minutes___ROSIE DAVIDSON

INGREDIENTS
2 grapefruits
4 oranges
1 pomegranate, halved
a little caster sugar
100g granola
10g mint leaves

METHOD
___Preheat a grill until very hot.
___Segment the grapefruits and oranges, keeping them separate. Tap the pomegranate seeds into a bowl (see page 52).
___Place the grapefruit on a baking tray, sprinkle evenly with caster sugar and place under the hot grill for two minutes, or until the sugar bubbles.
___Place on a serving dish and arrange around the orange, segments, pomegranate seeds, granola and mint.

___SPICED PLUMS in RED WINE___

Fragrant, rich and wonderful served warm with ice cream, or chilled for breakfast with thick yogurt.

SERVES 4–6___PREP 10 minutes___COOK 40 minutes___HUGH MERRILL

INGREDIENTS

500g plums

275ml red wine
   (Malbec, Shiraz or Syrah)

3 star anise

6 cloves

95g soft brown sugar

METHOD

___Preheat the oven to 170°C/fan 150°C/gas mark 3½.

___Cut the plums in half, pit them and place flat sides down in an ovenproof dish. Scatter the remaining ingredients evenly on top of the plums.

___Cook in the oven for 40 minutes. Serve hot or cold. This also reheats very successfully.

___LITTLE LIME POSSETS with CHILLI-TAMARIND CURD___

Addictive pots with an ethereal lightness. And you can make them the day before you want them.

SERVES 6–8___PREP 10 minutes___COOK 20 minutes___THOMASINA MIERS

INGREDIENTS

For the possets
500ml double cream
finely grated zest and juice of 5 large limes,
   plus more lime zest to serve
150g golden caster sugar
1 tsp vanilla extract

For the curd
1 egg, plus 3 egg yolks
finely grated zest and juice of 3 limes
4 tbsp tamarind paste
130g caster sugar
½ tsp chilli flakes
150g unsalted butter, cut into small cubes

METHOD

___To make the possets, put the cream, lime zest, caster sugar and vanilla extract in a saucepan and bring to the boil, stirring occasionally to dissolve the sugar. Reduce the heat and leave to bubble for a few minutes, stirring from time to time. Whisk in the lime juice, then remove from the heat. Pour the hot cream through a sieve into a jug, then decant into six to eight glasses and chill in the fridge.

___To make the curd, whisk the egg, egg yolks, lime zest and juice, tamarind, sugar and chilli together in a saucepan over a low heat, then whisk in the butter, a cube at a time. Let this curd cook for 10–15 minutes, stirring regularly, until it is thick and custard-like but, at the first sign of the mixture erupting with a 'plop', remove it from the heat. Strain the curd through a sieve into a clean bowl, cover and allow to cool.

___Spoon a layer of the curd over each of the set possets, return to the fridge and leave to set overnight. Serve topped with curls of zest and eat them either on their own, or with almond biscotti and a glass of aged tequila.

___This batch of curd is a little big for the recipe, so eat the leftovers on toast. Or double the recipe so that you have plenty: it's great with vanilla ice cream and will keep for a week in the fridge in a sealed container.

___QUICK CHOCOLATE CAKE___

The all-in-one method makes this ideal for the time-poor. Just leave time for the icing to set.

SERVES 8___PREP 10 minutes___COOK 40 minutes___EDWINA GROSVENOR

INGREDIENTS

For the cake
125ml vegetable oil,
　plus more for the tins
225g plain flour
350g caster sugar
85g cocoa powder
1½ tsp baking powder
2 large eggs
250ml milk
2 tsp vanilla extract
raspberries, to serve
　(optional)

For the icing
200g dark chocolate, broken
　into pieces
200ml double cream
chocolate curls, to serve
　(optional)

METHOD

___Preheat the oven to 180°C/fan 160°C/gas mark 4. Oil two 20cm sandwich tins and line their bases with circles of baking parchment.

___For the cake, place all the ingredients into a large bowl. Boil a kettle of water. Using a wooden spoon, or electric whisk, beat the mixture until smooth and well combined. Add 250ml of boiling water to the mixture, a little at a time, beating until smooth. (The mixture will now be very liquid.)

___Divide the batter between the sandwich tins and bake in the oven for 25–35 minutes, or until the tops are firm to the touch and a skewer inserted into the centre of a cake comes out clean. Remove the cakes from the oven and allow to cool completely, still in their tins, before icing.

___For the icing, heat the chocolate and cream in a saucepan over a low heat until the chocolate melts. Remove the pan from the heat and whisk the mixture until smooth, glossy and thickened. Set aside to cool for one to two hours, or until thick enough to spread over the cake.

___To assemble the cake, run a round-bladed knife around the inside of the cake tins to loosen them, then carefully remove from the tins. Spread the icing over the top of both of the cakes, adding a layer of raspberries too, if you like, then carefully stack one cake on top of the other. Transfer to a serving plate and sprinkle with chocolate curls, if you like.

___VANILLA CREAMED RICE with PEACHES___

You can serve this pudding warm or cold. It's lovely with a shortbread biscuit.

SERVES 4___PREP 10 minutes___COOK 35 minutes___ALBERT ROUX

INGREDIENTS
120g pudding rice
400ml whole milk
1 vanilla pod, split, seeds scraped out
50g caster sugar, plus a little more for the peaches
30ml double cream
100ml condensed milk
25g salted butter
2 ripe peaches

METHOD
____Rinse the rice well under cold running water and drain. Bring the milk to the boil together with the vanilla pod and seeds and the sugar, add the rice and simmer for 30 minutes, stirring occasionally.

____When soft, let it sit for five minutes off the heat, then stir in the cream, condensed milk and butter.

____Meanwhile, plunge the peaches into boiling water for 10 seconds, then remove with a slotted spoon and drop them straight into cold water. Remove from the water and peel off the skins.

____Cut each peach into six wedges. Poach them in a little water and sugar in a broad sauté pan, in a single layer, until tender but still holding their shape.

____Remove the vanilla pod from the creamed rice and serve it with the poached peaches.

___CHOCOLATE and TRIPLE HAZLENUT TART___

There are two parts to this, pastry and filling, but both are easy. Just leave time to chill the tart.

SERVES 6–8___PREP 10 minutes___COOK 30 minutes___PAUL CLARKSON

INGREDIENTS

For the pastry
100g unsalted butter
225g plain flour,
    plus more to dust
1 egg, lightly beaten
pinch of salt
100g blanched hazelnuts,
    ground
30g vanilla sugar, or
    1 tbsp caster sugar with
    1 tsp vanilla powder

For the filling
500ml double cream
75g vanilla sugar, or
    70g caster sugar with
    1 tsp vanilla powder
dash of flavourless oil, or
    hazelnut oil
100g blanched hazelnuts,
    skinned, plus more,
    crushed, to serve
100g dark chocolate
    (70% cocoa solids), broken
    into small pieces
50g cocoa powder
25g cornflour
100–120ml milk

METHOD

___Start with the pastry. Rub the butter into the flour with your fingertips, or in a food processor, until it looks like crumbs. Add the egg, salt, hazelnuts and sugar (or sugar and vanilla powder) and bring the mix together into a pastry. Wrap in cling film and chill in the fridge for 30 minutes.

___Preheat the oven to 180°C/fan 160°C/gas mark 4. Roll the pastry out on a lightly floured surface and use it to line a 23cm tart tin or flan ring. Cover with baking parchment and weigh down with baking beans, dried pulses or raw rice. Bake for 17 minutes, then remove the baking beans and paper and bake for a final three minutes. Allow to cool.

___For the filling, take a heavy-based saucepan and heat the cream. Add the sugar (or sugar and vanilla powder), oil, nuts and dark chocolate and heat very gently, stirring often, until the ingredients melt. Mix the cocoa, cornflour and milk together to make a smooth paste and add it to the simmering chocolate mix. Stir until it thickens (about eight minutes), then pour it into a bowl and allow to cool for 15 minutes.

___Pour the filling into the pastry case, cover and chill for at least four hours. Sprinkle with crushed hazelnuts and serve with cream.

___FRUIT SUNDAES___

A delicious, tart pudding for the complete non-cook.

SERVES 2___PREP 10 minutes___ANNIE FORT

INGREDIENTS
200g raspberries
50g strawberries, sliced
1 kiwi fruit, sliced
frozen yogurt or vanilla ice cream, to serve
2 sprigs of mint

METHOD
___Keeping back six nice-shaped raspberries, mash the rest in a bowl with a fork until smooth. Push through a sieve into a bowl, to remove the seeds.

___Divide most of the strawberries and kiwi between two dishes or glasses, with two scoops of yogurt or ice cream. Drizzle the raspberry purée over the top.

___Arrange the remaining strawberries and kiwi slices and reserved whole raspberries on top and decorate each sundae with a mint sprig.

___RICOTTA TART___

Completely delicious. You need fresh ricotta, not the widely available UHT variety.

SERVES 6–8___PREP 20 minutes___COOK 30 minutes___ANTONIO CARLUCCIO

INGREDIENTS

For the crust

50g unsalted butter, plus more for the tin

4 sheets of filo pastry (frozen)

For the filling

500g fresh ricotta cheese

120g caster sugar

5 eggs, separated

150g mix of candied orange and lemon peel, cut into small cubes

finely grated zest of 1 unwaxed lemon

50g dark chocolate, broken into small pieces

METHOD

___Preheat the oven to 180°C/fan 160°C/gas mark 4. Melt the butter in a saucepan over a low heat. Use a little of it to brush a 25cm tart tin. Line the tin with three sheets of the filo pastry, brushing each sheet with some more of the melted butter as you go.

___Put the ricotta in a bowl and loosen the texture with a fork. Mix in 100g of the sugar and the egg yolks, followed by the candied peel, grated zest and chocolate. Mix together well.

___In another bowl, beat the egg whites until stiff, then add the remaining sugar, still whisking. Fold this carefully into the ricotta mixture using a large metal spoon, taking care not to lose the airiness of the whipped whites.

___Spread this filling on to the pastry base. Brush melted butter over the remaining sheet of filo. With scissors, cut ribbons of buttered filo pastry and spread these decoratively on the tart.

___Bake in the oven for 30 minutes and leave to cool before serving.

___WHIZZY CHESTNUT WHIP___

Even your least culinarily gifted family member can handle this, as long as they can operate a can opener and have been briefed on how to work the food processor. Yum.

SERVES 6___PREP 5 minutes___JANE SANDERSON

INGREDIENTS
400g can of unsweetened
    chestnut purée
200g crème fraîche
125g golden caster sugar
1 tsp vanilla extract
1 tbsp dark rum (optional)

METHOD
___In a food processor, whizz all the ingredients until smooth.
___Divide between six serving pots. Cover and chill until required.
___That's it.
___Sprinkle with chocolate curls, if you like.

___AL'S BAKED PEACHES with HONEY and MASCARPONE___

Lovely even when you can't get good peaches; baking makes them sweet and juicy.

SERVES 2___PREP 5 minutes___COOK 20–30 minutes

INGREDIENTS

2 large ripe peaches,
   ideally white-fleshed
clear honey
100g mascarpone cheese
25g caster sugar
1 vanilla pod, split,
   seeds scraped out

METHOD

___Preheat the oven to 150°C/fan 130°C/gas mark 2. Halve the peaches and remove the stones. Place, hollow sides up, in a baking dish and drizzle with 1 tbsp of the honey. Bake for 20–30 minutes, or until completely tender.

___Blend the mascarpone with the sugar and vanilla seeds.

___Remove the peaches from the oven and drizzle with clear honey. Serve with the mascarpone on top or alongside.

___LOLLY'S UNBELIEVABLY GOOD BROWNIES___

So simple to throw together and always the first cake to disappear.

MAKES 16___PREP 15 minutes___COOK 25 minutes___JULIE PEASGOOD

INGREDIENTS
80g unsalted butter, plus more for the tin
250g dark chocolate, broken into pieces
75g plain flour
½ tsp baking powder
¼ tsp salt
2 eggs
240g caster sugar
1 tsp vanilla extract
75g chopped nuts (optional but really good)

METHOD
___Butter a 20cm square baking tin. Preheat the oven to 180°C/fan 160°C/gas mark 4.
___Place the chocolate in a heatproof bowl with the butter. Set it over a saucepan of simmering water (the bowl should not touch the water). Allow to melt, then set aside to cool slightly.
___Mix the flour with the baking powder and salt.
___With an electric whisk in a large bowl, beat the eggs well and then gradually beat in the sugar. Blend in the chocolate mixture and vanilla extract, then fold in the flour mixture. Add the nuts, if you want. Spread into the prepared tin.
___Bake for 25 minutes. Cool, cut into squares and serve with vanilla ice cream and hot chocolate sauce.

___SPICED BANANA MARSHMALLOWS___

You will need a sugar thermometer, but don't worry, these are easy and great fun.

MAKES 1kg___PREP 20 minutes___COOK 15 minutes___JULES HECKMAN HUGHES

INGREDIENTS
750g granulated sugar
35g gelatine leaves
3 egg whites
260g banana purée (blend about 3 bananas)
½ tsp mixed spice
½ tsp ground cinnamon
toasted desiccated coconut, to dust

METHOD
___Heat the sugar and 260ml of water in a heavy-based saucepan until the sugar dissolves, then heat the mixture to 125°C. Soak the gelatine in a small bowl of water to cover. Line a baking tray with cling film.
___Whisk the egg whites to medium peaks in a food mixer, then slowly drizzle in the hot syrup mix, whisking continually.
___Meanwhile, place the banana purée, mixed spice and cinnamon in a saucepan and warm, but do not boil. Remove the gelatine from the water and squeeze it out. Add to the purée, mix and allow to melt.
___Slowly pour the banana purée mix into the marshmallow, still whisking continually and continuing to whisk until the bottom of the bowl is just lukewarm. Pour into the prepared tray, then allow to cool and set.
___Cut into squares and coat in toasted coconut.

First published in Great Britain in 2016 by The Clink Trading

Copyright © The Clink Trading 2016

The right of The Clink Trading to be identified as the Author of the Work has been asserted in accordance with the Copyright, Designs and Patents Act 1988.

All rights reserved. No part of this publication may be reproduced, stored in a retrieval system, or transmitted, in any form or by any means, without the prior written permission of the publisher, nor be otherwise circulated in any form of binding or cover other than that in which it is published and without a similar condition being imposed on the subsequent purchaser.

A CIP catalogue record for this title is available from the British Library
ISBN 978 0 9933569 1 9

Publisher: Alison Cathie
Editor: Lucy Bannell
Photography and design: Ros Holder
Foreword (pages 4, 5 and 6) and jacket flap portrait photography: David Cummings
Home economist: Emily Jonzen
Proofreader: Joanne Murray
Indexer: Vicki Robinson
PR and marketing: Petra Clayton and Alexandra Bertram
Project manager: Christopher Moore

Printed and bound in China by 1010 Printing International Limited

The Clink Trading
HMP High Down
High Down Lane
Sutton
Surrey
SM2 5PJ
www.theclinkcharity.org

I would like to thank all those who have provided recipes and have helped in producing this, our second Clink recipe book. I would like to pay particular thanks to Albert Roux (Group Chef Ambassador) who has been a constant source of advice and inspiration to me and the team, also to the team at Custard Communications for their amazing work, and most importantly to Alison Cathie (Clink Publishing Ambassador) and her team for having coordinated and produced another wonderful publication.

Finlay Scott, Chairman

Other recipe contributors:
Sir William Atkinson: Clink Trustee
Antonio Carluccio: Clink Chef Ambassador
Paul Clarkson: Clink Head Chef, HMP Brixton
Rosie Davidson: Clink Trustee
Annie Fort: Clink General Manager, HMP High Down
Gary Gates: Clink Gardens Manager, HMP Send
Silvano Giraldin: Clink Restaurant Ambassador
Lady Edwina Grosvenor: Clink Founder Trustee
Jules Heckman Hughes: Clink Events Ambassador
Sadiq Khan: Mayor of London
Vic Laws: Clink Group Restaurant Ambassador
Giorgio Locatelli: Clink Chef Ambassador
Hugh Merrill: Clink Group Communications Ambassador
Kevin McGrath: Clink Founder Trustee
Thomasina Miers: Clink Chef Ambassador
Christopher Moore: Clink Chief Executive
Julie Peasgood: Clink Sustainability Ambassador
John Retallick: Clink Chef Ambassador
Albert Roux: Clink Group Chef Ambassador
Jane Sanderson: Clink Director of Operations
Finlay Scott: Clink Founder Trustee
Sally Scott: Clink Friend
Matt Tebbutt: Clink Chef Ambassador
Tim Wates: Clink Trustee
Debbie Whitworth: Clink Finance Director

Recipes on pages 43 and 92 © Thomasina Miers from Chilli Notes by Thomasina Miers (Hodder & Stoughton)